Labor Unions
In The United States of America

Louis Bevoc

I0503261

Published by
NutriNiche System LLC

Louis Bevoc books...simple explanations of complex subjects

Introduction

Before beginning, it is important to note that this book does not support or oppose unions in workplaces, nor does it argue any position on the topic. It is written for readers to gain a better understanding of union functions, ideals, structures, activities, and history. It makes a concerted effort not to be biased so readers can gather factual information and form their own opinions about the organizing of workforces.

When an association of United States workers forms a legal unit for bargaining purposes, that unit is known as a labor union. Labor unions, also referred to as unions, give power to the people who are a part of them so those people have a say in their financial well-being rather than leaving it up to government officials or management personnel.

Unions typically negotiate wages, benefits, working conditions, and worker rights in what is known as collective bargaining. Collective bargaining is described below for a better understanding of what it does, who it involves, and how it functions.

Collective bargaining

Any old saying states, "beauty is in the eye of the beholder." In other words, the beauty of something is dependent on who is observing it. This saying has application in workplaces all over the United States except the word "beauty" is replaced with "fairness." When it comes to determining compensation of employees, fairness truly is dependent on who is observing. Typically, management personnel view things differently than employees, and that is why collective bargaining came into being.

The term "collective bargaining" was coined in the early 1890s by an English sociologist named Beatrice Web. Ms. Web was a major player in Britain's industrial revolution and she was also a founder of the London School of Economics. Her work was instrumental for the development of processes that helped workers get paid a fair wage for the work they were performing. This marked the end for management setting employees' wages based solely on what they believed the workers should earn.

Not surprisingly, workers in the United States saw what was happening in Britain and began to voice their opinions about management having complete control over employee wages. They wanted to have a say in what was considered "fair" pay and this led to them protesting against the management of the companies that employed them. These protests, along with the help of politicians who took the side of the workers, led to a 1935 act that covered most private sector collective bargaining agreements. This act, known as the National Labor Relations Act, makes it illegal for employers to discriminate or harass employees due to their union membership or organizing activities. It also gave employees the right to engage in collective bargaining and strike if they believe they are being mistreated. In a nutshell, the act was put into law to correct the inequality of bargaining power (where one party has more effective alternatives than the other) between employers and employees by promoting collective bargaining between trade unions and employers. However, it should be noted that this act also made it illegal to make joining a union a requirement for becoming an employee.

What exactly is meant by collective bargaining? Collective bargaining is a negotiation process designed to reach an agreement between workers and their employers on employee compensation (usually pay and benefits) and other work-related matters such as work-life balance and minimum work hour guarantees. Typically, employers are represented by management officials and employees are represented by the union that they belong to. Each side also has specialized attorneys and other personnel present at the negotiation who offer support and information for their clients to use as leverage for their position.

The amount of time required to complete collective bargaining negotiations varies based on the situation. It can take days, weeks, or months depending on the demands of the contract and the rules that are in place. However, employers have a legal obligation to bargain in "good faith" with their employees, and they cannot engage in tactical stalls. In other words, they must be willing to reach an agreement, respond to proposals on time, and avoid undermining the bargaining process.

So, in a nutshell, collective bargaining is a formal process that involves employers and employees (typically represented by unions) negotiating with each other to establish wages, conditions, terms, policies, procedures, actions, and other matters related to work. Attorneys and other specialized personnel for each side are involved and the time for completion varies based on the importance of the topics under debate. However, negotiations eventually end and the result is a collective bargaining agreement that is binding to management and labor. This agreement is usually clear and fairly detailed, but, if disputes arise, then they are typically resolved via mediation or arbitration following specific procedures found in the collective bargaining agreement.

Now you understand a little about unions and what collective bargaining entails. Let's move forward to the next section that shows how union leadership aligns the unions they represent with larger entities for structure and power.

Alignment

Unions in the United States typically align with one of two larger organizations that promote policies designed to help the workers obtain higher wages and benefits while maintaining a good work-life balance. The larger organizations are known as the AFL-CIO and the Change to Win Federation, both of which are described below for a better understanding of how they were established and what they do.

AFL-CIO

The American Federation of Labor and Congress of Industrial Organizations (AFL–CIO) was formed in the mid-1950s when the AFL and CIO merged. Membership grew steadily until the late 1970s, but that was the heyday and present membership is only about 60 percent of what it was back then. This decline is partially due to fewer unionized companies, but it is also because several large unions broke away in 2005 to form the Change to Win Federation. However, the AFL-CIO is still the biggest federation of unions that exists in the United States. It consists of over fifty unions (national and international) and represents millions of workers, some of whom are actively employed and others who are retired.

The AFL-CIO is overseen and regulated by the member unions within it. Delegates represent each union based on numbers that are proportional to membership. In a nutshell, these delegates elect officers, set agendas, approve policies and procedures, and establish dues that all members are required to pay. Officers consist of the president, executive vice-president, and secretary-treasurer, and their terms are limited to four years.

The AFL-CIO has liberal tendencies and is supportive of the Democratic Party. This affiliation should not be surprising to anyone who understands politics because the democrats push for a progressive agenda and have a strong base of liberal members. These politicians also tend to side with the needs and demands of the people who work for organizations, AKA the employees, rather than the people who own and operate them, AKA the management.

One might think that the AFL-CIO dictates the actions of the unions that fall under its umbrella. This thinking, however, is not true and the reality is that this federation has limited input or jurisdiction on management agendas. Other than corruption issues or major disagreements, they remain in the background and let the unions set their own rules and regulations.

Change to Win Federation

As mentioned earlier, the Change to Win Federation (CTW) was formed in 2005 when several large unions broke away from the AFL-CIO. CTW is a coalition of United States unions that adheres to the organizing model which is described below for a better understanding of its function.

Organizing model

This model shows how unions should recruit and promote the interests of their members. It requires a lot of organizing and networking to be successful, and its tactics can be quite confrontational and eye-opening. Present-day members spend a good deal of time trying to minimize or reverse the current trend of declining membership so unions can reclaim the power and status that they possessed in the not-so-distant past.

The goal of the organizing model is to let the members control the direction of the union. Organizing campaigns revolve around talking to potential members about their current situations and discussing ways that those situations can be improved. Interpersonal relationships with workers are the key to the model's success, and organizing takes place in the "workplace trenches" to form those relationships.

Not surprisingly, the organizing model works best when many supporters are involved. These supporters build the confidence of workers while acting as sounding boards for questions and concerns. Once the workers are convinced that unionization is the way to go, they do a lot to further the cause because their pro-union actions become contagious.

The organizing model allows CTW to promote its agenda while leaving a lasting impression on the workers they recruit. Two basic principles are as follows:

- Membership must constantly increase with the goal being the addition of millions of more people.
- Every worker has the right to a union that has the resources and strategy to fight for their rights, wages, and welfare.

The objectives of the CTW are also very important because they form the basis of the federation's entire system. These objectives include those listed below.

- Encourage unions to organize within industries.
- Consolidate small unions into large unions.
- Invest money into new membership rather than politics.
- Recruit women, minorities, and people of color.
- Move away from traditional manufacturing unionization.

The last two objectives listed above are of particular interest because they are critical for the overall survival of unions. The recruitment of women, minorities, and people of color has to be a top priority because workplace demographics have changed considerably over the past few decades. Organizing activities with any type of exclusivity are destined for failure because employee ranks are no longer dominated by one race or gender and workplace diversity is most likely going to increase in the future.

The last objective, moving away from manufacturing recruiting, is also critical because manufacturing as we knew it in the past no longer exists. Quite simply, job composition (which will be discussed in more detail later in this book) has changed causing many of the manufacturing jobs that were once plentiful to reduce in numbers or, in the worst-case scenarios, disappear.

Since its inception, the CTW has been involved with many different types of union campaigns. From truck drivers to phone service providers, they have supported a variety of unionizing efforts. However, their most well-known organizing work is probably the "fight for $15" movement which advocates raising the federal minimum wage to $15 per hour. The movement focuses on employees working in traditionally lower-paying jobs such as those found in child care, home healthcare, convenience stores, and fast-food restaurants to increase their wages and help them form labor unions.

Regardless of the alignment of unions, they share a common goal of making life better for their members. Based on this philosophy, one might think that the majority of employees would be enticed to join unions. However, that does not appear to be the case as unions represent less than 20 percent of the entire United States workforce, with the private sector accounting for less than half of that representation. Interestingly, union membership has not been this low in the private sector in over three-quarters of a century.

The most visible and well-known unions are found in the public sector. This is interesting because compensation is relatively the same for union and non-union employees in the public sector so unions do not appear to be needed. The government pays close attention to employee wages to assure that employees are paid equally for the jobs that they perform while taking into account the geographical areas where they are employed. However, regardless of governmental monitoring of worker pay, some employees still prefer to be part of a union. They might feel that their jobs are more secure under the protection of the union or they might just want to be part of a union but, regardless of the reason, they become union members and remain that way for their entire careers.

The public sector is made up of public services and public enterprises and includes governmental services such as police forces and branches of the military. Unlike the private sector, many of the goods and services provided by the public sector are available to everyone regardless of whether or not they pay for them. Paved roads, water supply, and street lights are examples of services that are available to everyone (other than extreme cases such as people in prison) who wants to use them. Think about the fact that a person who lives, works, and pays taxes in Shreveport, Louisiana can consume as much water as they want at a drinking fountain in San Francisco, California free of charge. They can then drive hundreds of miles on beautifully paved scenic oceanside highways at night while the road is illuminated by free street lights.

Most people take for granted the goods and services provided by the public sector since they have enjoyed them at relatively no cost for their entire lives. However, the same cannot be said about the workers who are employed in this sector. They take their wage and benefit compensation very seriously, and they become members of unions to improve upon that compensation while finding a balance between their jobs and family lives.

Like it or not, union representation in the United States has declined in somewhat significant numbers over the past three decades. Many people wonder why this decrease has taken place after unions have been shown to provide higher wages and better benefits for members when compared to non-union organizations. While wages and benefits are comparable for union workers in the public sector, statistics show that union workers in the private sector experience compensation that is more than ten percent higher than non-union employees.

Some of the reasons for the decline in union membership in the public sector and private sector are discussed below.

Anti-organizing activities

Companies in the private sector are fighting harder than they ever have in the past to prevent their employees from unionizing. Leaders know that unions fight for higher compensation for employees and the bottom lines of their organizations will be impacted by any increases. They also know that unions affect management strategies because unions are more interested in the well-being of their members than they are in the profitability of the organizations that employ those members. This is not saying that union officials do not think about profits because they understand that profits are needed for survival. It is merely saying that the main focus of a union is the people within it.

There are laws regarding what cannot be done by companies when fighting against organizing efforts. Many of these laws are designed to prevent intimidation, threats, and other coercion tactics that were used in the past to prevent unions from getting in the door, and violation of them could lead to companies being subjected to unfair labor practices. Other laws were designed to prevent employers from making promises for favors or spying on their workers to get information.

Examples of illegal actions by companies include those listed below.

Promising perks – It is illegal to promise employees special benefits for trying to stop the union from organizing. For example, the owner of a company cannot promise to pay for an employee's home lawn care and snow removal service if he spreads bad words about the union.

Threatening job loss or plant closures – It is illegal to threaten people with any type of financial hardship if they bring in the union. For example, management cannot tell the employees that the plant will shut down if they vote in the union.

Spying on employee meetings – Employees are allowed to meet and talk about the union without fear of management spying on them or inserting spies to report what is being discussed. For example, a CEO cannot hire a person to attend employee meetings and gather information about union activities.

Laying off or terminating employees – It is illegal to threaten employees with any type of job loss because they are involved with unions. For example, a manager cannot tell an employee that she will be fired if she talks to union representatives about organizing the workforce.

Giving incentive raises or bonuses – Management cannot give a raise or bonus as a means of motivating employees to work against a union. For example, the president of a company cannot give 10 percent raises to all hourly personnel after she finds out that they are talking to a union about becoming members.

The above examples show what a company cannot do to prevent a union from organizing the workforce. However, they are allowed to take some action including the following:

Discuss past experiences – Managers can discuss the experiences that have had with unions in the past...providing those experiences are factual. These types of discussions can be very helpful to those opposing union representation because they expose the bad things that can happen when workforces are organized. If done correctly, examples of past negative experiences can be the most powerful tool available to management personnel because they indicate what kind of things really do happen, regardless of what workers are told by union representatives.

Compare union and non-union compensation – This type of action is of little or no value if a company does not compete with union wages and benefits. However, it is very valuable if the company is competitive with the compensation that union employees in similar organizations receive. Management can show the employees that they might not gain anything by becoming members of the union. They can also tell workers that their compensation might be lowered due to the dues that they will be required to pay.

Correct false statements – Leaders of organizations do not have to sit back and watch their reputation be destroyed by inaccurate or untrue statements. They are allowed to fight back by stating the facts and correcting anything said by the union that might be misleading. False statement correction is important because lies and inaccuracies can cause employees to vote for the union based on things that are not true.

Talk about requirements – Management can tell employees that they will be paying dues if they join a union while reminding them that they are not currently paying any type of dues. Management can also tell the workers that they will need to abide by a new set of rules established by the union and violation of those rules could result in fines; thereby costing them more money out of their pockets.

Hire outside expertise – Some consultants help companies avoid workforce unionization by talking to the employees about the negative realities of membership. These individuals understand the subject matter and know what they can and cannot say and do without subjecting the company to unfair labor practice claims. Some consultants were union members or union leaders before they decided to work against them so they understand the entire organizing effort. In many organizing situations, consultants are well worth the investment...especially if management lacks understanding of how unions operate.

It should be noted that the anti-organizing efforts of companies are not always bad for employees. Company leaders are forced to realize that they need to pay employees higher wages to prevent them from unionizing, so they open up their wallets. Workers are rewarded for their efforts in the hope that they will not have any interest in organizing the workforce.

Job composition

Job composition refers to the types of jobs that make up workplaces. Manufacturing made up a high percentage of the jobs that were available in the past, especially following the industrial revolution, but this has changed to meet the demands of the new world. The lower percentage of manufacturing jobs today has impacted many aspects of the workforce...including the unionization of employees.

Unions have traditionally had a stronghold on the manufacturing segment of the private sector. Not all plants are unionized, but it is rare that production employees will not, at the very least, entertain organizing attempts to see if joining a union would benefit them. History has shown that plant workers usually welcome organizing efforts to improve the wages they earn and the environments they work in.

Warm receptions toward organizing efforts are still the norm at many manufacturing facilities; thereby allowing unions to maintain employee membership. However, over the past forty years, manufacturing jobs have decreased due to downsizing, technology, and lack of necessity. Cost factors have resulted in companies reducing or eliminating some of the plant jobs that were once plentiful. The luxury of having backup workers for the labor force is long gone as eroded profit margins have forced companies to become leaner. Some manufacturers hire temporary workers to fill jobs so they do not have to pay the benefits associated with full-time employment. When employees are in temporary positions, it is even more difficult for unions to organize them.

Technology has also impacted union efforts because manufacturing employees can be replaced by machines. Robots can do the work of people more effectively and efficiently....and they do not require breaks, file grievances, or ask for better wages and benefits.   Shareholders can be very demanding and, unfortunately, they are often more concerned with returns on their investments than they are with the economic well-being of laborers.

Fear of job loss

Some people think that job loss due to the unionizing of a workforce is nothing more than a threat. After all, management in a company is not going to sacrifice their financial well-being just because they have to give a portion of their earnings away to the workers. Additionally, it is illegal to threaten workers with job loss or shutdowns when a union is trying to organize the workforce. However, there is an unfortunate chance that job loss will be a direct consequence of some unionizing situations. Rather than submit to the demands of a union, some organizations relocate to less union-friendly areas or, in worst-case scenarios, close their doors.

If company leadership chooses to shut down due to a union, it is not likely due to their hatred of unions or desire to see organizing attempts fail. It is more likely due to their belief that they cannot meet the financial demands of the union and stay in business. Quite simply, they think that wage and benefit increases in the workforce will make it difficult for the company to compete so they decide to "throw in the towel" rather than fight a losing battle.

Job loss is not always a consequence of union activities, and it is likely one of the lesser factors for the trending decrease in the unionization of workforces. However, it is a reality in some situations and it does cause people to think twice about becoming union members.

Wage and benefit costs

It is a known fact that unionized workforces are typically better compensated than similar non-unionized workforces. Union workers receive higher wages and better benefits for the same, and sometimes even less, work. However, employees are starting to find that higher compensation might not be permanent because union demands sometimes push companies to a breaking point where they are forced to shut down or move the jobs to areas where unions lack power or do not exist.

The hardest hit from compensation increases typically does not come from wages. Instead, it results from benefits such as health care and retirement plans. Health care costs to organizations tend to increase every year, and it becomes more and more difficult for them to absorb those increases. If unions refuse to let some of the costs be passed on to their members, then a breaking point could come about.

In terms of retirement plans, 401K plans are somewhat affordable. However, some unions in the public sector still seek pension plans which are becoming continuously more expensive to fund. Quite simply, people are living longer today than they ever have in the past, and retirees' expenses can no longer be covered by the companies that employed them or the contributions of union members who are still working.

Now you have an understanding of the basic concept of unions, collective bargaining, affiliations with the AFL-CIO and CTW, and reasons for recent declines in membership. These aspects of union representation provide a good background for the next section that discusses specific types of unions found in the United States.

Types

As noted early, union membership has declined since the mid-20th century. However, unions still hold power and they influence the way many organizations operate and conduct business.

Essentially, there are three major types of unions in the United States. These unions are described and exemplified below.

Industrial

Industrial unions generally represent workers in specific industries, regardless of the jobs they perform. They have more members than craft unions because craft unions are limited to individual trades or skills.

Types of industries that elect industrial unions include:

- *Transportation*
- *Distribution*
- *Warehousing*
- *Construction*
- *Food*
- *Chemical*
- *Power*

Industrial unions are considered better unions than craft unions due to the following:

- Industrial unions have greater bargaining power during contract negotiations because they have more members than craft unions.
- Industrial unions have more leverage during strikes because they have more members than craft unions.
- Industrial unions remain united at all times. This is not the case for craft unions because they are most concerned about the well-being of their members.

- Industrial unions are not divided. Craft unions tend to fight over jurisdiction and the right to strike.
- Industrial union members do not cross picket lines. Craft union members often have the freedom to cross each other's picket lines. In fact, some craft union contracts require members to cross picket lines of other unions.

Craft

Craft unions typically represent workers in a specific trade or occupation. This includes workers in skilled trades.

Occupations that elect craft unions include:

- Electricians
- Millwrights
- Plumbers
- Welders
- Pipefitters
- Machinists

Craft unions are considered better unions than industrial unions due to the following:

- Craft unions can get higher wagers for specifically skilled workers. Industrial unions have to negotiate the group as a whole, so skilled workers lose to compensate unskilled workers.
- Craft unions fight harder for every worker because memberships are smaller. Industrial unions have

large memberships and workers might not get left out.

- Craft unions control apprenticeships, and they can create a shortage of skilled workers to drive up wages. Industrial unions do not have apprenticeships to control, and they cannot drive up wages by creating shortages of workers.
- Craft unions control apprenticeships, and they can select the best individuals to assure the union continues. Industrial unions do not have apprentices to control, and they cannot select the best individuals to assure the union continues.
- Craft unions control the content of jobs and the skills needed to perform those jobs. Industrial unions cannot control the content or skills of their member's jobs.

Public sector

This is the largest type of union in the United States. It represents government workers, regardless of their job.

Workers in public sector unions include:

- Police officers
- Firefighters
- Postal workers
- Sanitation workers
- Teachers

Public sector unions are considered better unions than industrial unions or craft unions due to the following:

- Contract negotiations are based on government budgets...and governments rarely ever go bankrupt or shut down. Craft union and industrial union negotiations are based on the financial stability of private corporations...and private corporations go bankrupt and shut down regularly.
- Public sector unions have national exposure and often get public support or sympathy nationwide. Craft unions and industrial unions rarely get public support or sympathy on a national level.
- Public sector unions are growing in membership as craft unions and industrial unions decline in membership. This gives public sector unions more negotiating power than craft unions or industrial unions.

Now that you have an understanding of the three basic types of unions, let's move into the general structure of unions.

Structure

Unions have similar structures, but those structures are tailored toward the goals and objectives of the specific union. For example, a craft union for teachers would have a mission that is different from that of an industrial union in a food processing plant. The teachers' union might have a goal of reducing class sizes, while the food processing union wants to add more employees to the workforce.

Along the same lines, a police officers' public sector union would have a different mission than an electricians' craft union. The police officers' union might have a goal of increasing protective equipment for officers on the streets, while the electricians' union has the objective of eliminating holiday work.

Unions of the same type can also have differing objectives. Consider two types of occupations in the public sector unions - firefighters and sanitation workers. The firefighters' union might want members to work a maximum of one weekend per month, while the sanitation workers' union wants to reduce the maximum weight of refuse they are required to lift from 40 pounds to 35 pounds.

In short, the goals and philosophies of different unions reflect the needs of their members. However, the structure of all unions can be broken down into four major areas. These areas include the general membership, executive board, executive officers, and committees. Each area is described below and broken down into smaller components for a more detailed understanding.

General membership

General members are the reason unions are formed. They are the beneficiaries of union activity, and their needs rank above all other concerns. They are also the most powerful decision-making force within the union, and they control their destiny. However, this power comes with responsibilities that involve understanding union objectives and getting involved with union actions.

Below is a closer examination of the role of general membership within the union:

Benefits

- They are entitled to union education and training.
- They are entitled to union grievance support.
- They are entitled to union legal assistance when necessary.

Power

- They elect people to important union positions including the executive board and executive officers.
- They approve policies and procedures regarding union management.
- They approve changes in union leadership.

Responsibilities

- They need to understand the by-laws and constitution of the union.
- They need to participate in internal and external union activities.
- They need to pay dues for their union membership.

Executive board

This is the next level up from general membership on the union's hierarchical ladder. Members at this level make sure that approved policies and procedures are implemented and carried out in the manner designated by the general members.

The executive board plays an important role in the union because it ensures the general member's wishes are adhered to properly. Without this board, the guidelines voted in by general members would be essentially useless, and anarchy could be the result.

Additionally, the executive board considers the general members to be shareholders in the union. Like a board of directors in a business, they report on all union activities so general members are kept abreast of internal and external happenings.

Executive officers

This group consists of the president, vice-president, secretary, treasurer, auditors, chief steward, and stewards. Once elected by the general members, they are responsible for the daily functioning of the union. This entails being involved in virtually every aspect of daily operations to assure the union works for members to attain higher wages, better benefits, and improved working conditions.

Each officer has specific responsibilities regarding union operations, and those responsibilities are as follows:

President

The president is the main person responsible for the daily operations of the union. If the union is not achieving designated goals or objectives, then the president is responsible. In short, the president is accountable for the union's maintenance, growth, and prosperity.

Other responsibilities of the president often include:

- Acts as chief external union communicator
- Acts as chief internal union communicator
- Acts as chief union negotiator
- Acts as chief union arbitrator
- Oversees union executive board meetings
- Oversees union finances (P&L, budgets, expenses, etc.)
- Directs union executive officers
- Directs union general membership
- Signs all-important union documents

Vice-president

Similar to the vice-president of the United States, the vice-president assumes the president's responsibilities if he or she is unable to do so. He or she also handles other tasks assigned by the president.

Other responsibilities of the vice-president often include:

- Acts as chair of the grievance committee
- Acts as advisor to chief steward and stewards
- Coordinates union benefits
- Coordinates union training

Secretary

The secretary is responsible for all clerical duties. This involves maintaining and storing all records, files, and data related to union activities.

Other responsibilities of the secretary often include:

- Writes or records minutes at union meetings. Minutes are official records of union actions that are permanently maintained on file.
- Writes official union letters.
- Opens union mail (letter, bills, etc.) and delivers to appropriate officers

Treasurer

The treasurer handles many financial aspects of the union's daily operations. He or she monitors union funds for accuracy and discrepancies and maintains all financial transaction records. In short, the treasurer is a safeguard for union funds.

Other responsibilities of the treasurer often include:

- Prepares budget
- Manages assets
- Assures dues are collected
- Arranges for audits

Auditor

The auditor conducts audits of union financial activities over specific time periods. This assures that monetary transactions are consistent with the goals and objectives of the union. In short, the auditor is a safeguard for making sure union finances reflect the goals of the organization.

Specific aspects of union financial activities examined during an audit often include:

- Wages
- Expense reports
- Credit card charges
- Allowances
- Receipts
- Disbursements
- Government reports
- Union reports
- Record maintenance

Chief steward

A chief steward assists lower-level stewards in their daily activities. These individuals are typically seasoned union officials, and they serve the role of a mentor.

Other responsibilities of the chief steward often include:

- Educates new stewards on handling grievances
- Identifies member concerns and creates plans of action for addressing
- Oversees steward committee meetings

Steward

The steward is on the front line for member grievances. These individuals receive the grievances and process them using the standard union protocol.

Other responsibilities of the steward often include:

- Educates members on union policies and procedures
- Organizes union meetings with members
- Serves as union contact for disputes with company management

Committees

Unions have a variety of committees that utilize members from all levels of the hierarchy. These committees have different functions, but essentially they are designed to provide members with guidance, direction, and understanding in regard to union policies and procedures.

The following are examples of committees that are often formed by unions:

Organizing committee - This committee coordinates the efforts of the organizing process. It involves employees at all levels of the union, and it requires member commitment.

Education and training committee - This committee educates members on union programs, policies, and procedures. In short, it educates employees on their rights and responsibilities as union members.

Budget/finance committee - This committee serves as a watchdog over union money to assure it is used appropriately.

Legal Committee - This committee is in charge of any legal actions that take place within the union.

Information committee - This committee provides the union with the information needed for negotiations. Members gather facts and data that can be used to support the union's position.

Negotiation committee - This committee represents the union in negotiations with management. They establish goals based on the feedback they receive from members.

Grievance committee - This committee works to resolve disputes and conflicts between members and management.

Community services committee - This committee gets the union involved in the community to support the causes they deem worthwhile.

Retirees committee - This committee has a dual purpose. First, it organizes retirees to gain their support for the union. Then it gives back to the retirees by supporting community service programs that they value.

Now that you understand the structure of a union, it is time to move forward to another important aspect known as negotiation.

Negotiation

Negotiation skills are critical for union leaders and their representatives. Without them, members could suffer consequential wage and benefit losses that are difficult, if not impossible, to recoup. In short, the importance of negotiation skills cannot be overlooked, and that is why they warrant discussion in this book.

Negotiation is a process where people settle their differences by reaching an agreement. The goal is to reach that agreement with compromise from both sides. There will be some disagreement, but arguing should be minimal with the focus being on principle rather than position.

Negotiation is important because conflicts arise due to different viewpoints, wants, and needs. Without it, people would argue to no end, dislike each other, and be dissatisfied. Negotiation allows people to reach agreements that satisfy everyone involved. This does not mean that people will get exactly what they want. It means that they will get some things they want while compromising on others. If done correctly, negotiation creates a win-win situation.

Win-win situations are almost always better than win-lose situations, but it must also be remembered that the goal of each party is to negotiate an outcome that is best for their interests. This thinking can be applied to negotiation in organizations. For example, a union wants what is best for its members while management wants what is best for the company.

Negotiation occurs in organizations for a variety of reasons. When conflicts arise, they need to be resolved...and negotiation is the best process to achieve that resolution. Without some type of negotiation process, warring factions never cease. This negatively impacts workplaces in terms of growth and prosperity, and it can lead to an organization's demise. Union officials understand the importance of negotiation, and they take it very seriously. They also make sure that the people doing their negotiating have the necessary skills to get the job done.

Negotiation skills evolve from many different factors. All of these factors cannot be discussed in the scope of this book, but some of the major ones for union negotiators are listed below.

Planning

This might be the most important factor because planning prepares union negotiators for the entire negotiating process. Well-planned negotiations have a much better chance of being successful than poorly planned negotiations.

Planning involves:

> *Determining goals and objectives* - Know your objectives and the other party's objectives. Think about ideal

outcomes, acceptable outcomes, and unacceptable outcomes to the negotiation.

Conducting research - Learn as much as possible about the other party. Try to figure out what techniques and ideas can be used to influence their thinking. Also, try to find similar negotiations and examine the outcomes for possible relationships.

Defining information limitations - Determine the information that can be revealed to the other party and the information that needs to be kept confidential. This is important because some information can be used by the other party to strengthen their leverage in the negotiation process.

Preparing an agenda - Decide the order in which issues need to be discussed. Sometimes the least significant concerns are discussed first to lead up to the more important ones, and other times the opposite occurs so the most important issues are discussed first. The order depends on the agenda...and that is why the agenda needs to be planned.

The best way for union negotiators to think about planning is to remember the old saying, "Those who fail to plan, plan to fail."

Assuming

Union negotiators should never assume something is fact. In other words, avoid any type of bias during the negotiation. Try to find out exactly what the other party is looking for in the outcome. For example, school administrators might assume that a teacher's union is trying to negotiate higher wages for their members when the union's actual goal is to prevent a loss of benefits.

Asking

Union negotiators should avoid aggressive statements, ask open-ended questions, and focus on the other party's interests. Examples of these are as follows:

Aggressive vs. non-aggressive

Incorrect: This does not benefit union members in any way.
Correct: How is this beneficial to the union?

Closed-ended vs. open-ended

Incorrect: Are wages management's major concern?
Correct: What are management's major concerns?

Focus on one's own party vs. focus on the other party

Incorrect: The proposed health insurance plan is good for the union because we save money.
Correct: The proposed health insurance plan is good for management because you have more options.

Understanding

Identify the reason for the negotiation, isolate the problems involved, and pinpoint areas for compromise. Union negotiators who fail to understand these aspects of negotiation waste time and frustrate the other party.

Listening

Unfortunately, many people would rather hear themselves speak than listen to others. During negotiations, union representatives who are speaking cannot listen to what is being said by the other party....and they miss hearing important information that could be used to reach a compromise.

Listening is a learned skill that is often more important than speaking during negotiation. Maybe this is why people are born with two ears and only one mouth!

Observing

Similar to listening, observation is an important skill for union negotiators. Watch the other party's gestures and reactions to determine if they are nervous, excited, or upset. Non-verbal communication provides a wealth of information that can be used to reach a compromise.

Actions often speak louder than words. It's simply a matter of interpreting those actions.

Communicating

Communication is necessary for preventing misunderstanding. Union negotiators must convey their desired goals and the reasons why those goals are justifiable, and this is done through effective communication with the other party. Without effective communication, negotiations become confusing and frustrating...and compromises sometimes fail to be reached.

Controlling

This refers to controlling emotions. Union negotiators need to control their emotions during negotiations or they risk failing to achieve their objectives. Unfortunately, this is not always easy to do because negotiations can bring out frustration, irritation, anger, happiness, relief, joy, and many other feelings related to emotions...especially if the discussion gets personal.

It is always best to keep emotions in check during negotiations. While this can be difficult, it is possible. Sometimes all it takes is the practice that comes with experience.

Deciding

People need to be able to make decisions during negotiations. Wishy-washy union negotiators waste valuable time and often upset the other party in the process. This skill is especially important for compromising because opportunities arise instantaneously...and they disappear just as quickly.

One good thing about decision-making is the fact that it gets better with experience. Being involved in this aspect of a negotiation pays dividends the next time around.

The above skills are important for union negotiators, but they also need to use tactics to achieve the goals of their members. The following are some effective tactics that are very useful for negotiating purposes:

Offering

This tactic involves making the first offer. It's very difficult to determine which party should make the first offer in a negotiation. However, one rule to follow is to never make the first offer without knowing the real value of the subject being negotiated. For example:

> Union negotiators know that the average wage in their industry is $15 per hour, so they make the first offer of $17.50 per hour. This makes sense because they know where they want the wages to end up. They know the situation and their tactic of making the first offer is justified.

Bartering

This tactic involves trading one incentive for another to reach an agreement. For example:

> Management at a manufacturing plant is negotiating a new contract with the union. The plant only needs 11 millwrights based on production volume, but the union wants to maintain the jobs of the current 15 millwrights. Management agrees to keep the 15 jobs open in

exchange for the union allowing the millwrights' wages to be frozen for the next three years.

In this case, the tactic of bartering was successful because each party believed they accomplished their goals.

Waiting

This tactic involves patience. Specifically, it refers to union negotiators waiting before responding to an offer. It uses time to show that (1) there is no urgency and (2) other options are available. It also keeps the other side wondering if they offered enough incentive to reach an agreement.

Sectioning

Some negotiations fall apart because one or both of the parties refuse to compromise. They take an "all or nothing" approach and fail to reach an agreement. When this happens, both parties walk away unhappy.

A tactic used to deal with an "all or nothing" situation involves breaking the negotiations into smaller sections and dealing with each section on an individual basis. For example:

Management at a food processing company is in contract negotiations with the union representing truck drivers. One of the issues is that the union does not want drivers to work on Sundays because they need time to be with their families. However, management must have drivers work on Sunday because products need to reach the stores daily.

Both parties are unwilling to budge on this issue, so they decide to separately work on another area of the contract. They discuss the wage and benefit packages for the drivers and reach an agreement that out-of-pocket insurance costs will not rise for the next two years and wages will be limited to a three percent increase. This agreement does not resolve the Sunday work issue, but it completes the wage and benefit part of the contract negotiation.

In this case, the tactic of sectioning allowed the parties to reach an agreement on a certain aspect of the negotiation, and it helped everyone feel like some progress was being made toward a resolution.

Prioritizing

This tactic establishes important aspects of the negotiation process including:

Separating business from personal

This expands upon the controlling factor discussed in the skills section. Union negotiators need to focus on facts rather than their emotions. Emotional reactions can be very strong and work against the goals and objectives trying to be achieved. This is why business facts need to be prioritized over personal feelings during negotiations.

Determining issue significance

Issues are sometimes placed in order of importance to establish agendas that have the best chance of achieving goals and objectives. This allows union negotiators to give more attention to top priorities in the beginning. For example:

> Hourly wages are the most important concern for fast food workers, so they are discussed first and foremost during contract negotiations. Issues related to health care and paid holidays take a back seat until the wages aspect is resolved.

Taking the reins

This involves union representatives taking control of the agenda for the negotiations. Location, size of the room, time limits, and the number of negotiators all fall into this category. Some of these factors might not seem significant, but they can play an important role. It's comparable to a home-field advantage for a sports team.

Questioning

This expands upon the asking factor discussed in the skills section. Union negotiators should ask questions rather than make concrete statements that result in arguments. For example:

> Incorrect: Your offer is completely useless to the union members.

Correct: Can you tell me how your offer benefits to the union members?

Incorrect: This will work well for management.
Correct: Will this work well for management?

Incorrect: Management does not understand the union's offer.
Correct: Would you like me to clarify the union's offer?

Always remember that questions open people up for discussion, and concrete statements shut them down.

Walking

This tactic is used by union officials when the negotiation process fails and an agreement cannot be reached. Typically a future meeting is scheduled for further negotiation. This allows both sides to rethink their position and come back to the table with a new or different perspective.

The walking tactic should be a last resort. However, it works well to prevent:

- Heated arguments that result when negotiators disagree
- Wasted time that results when negotiators disagree
- Damaged working relationships that result when negotiators disagree

The above tactics are beneficial for reaching agreements, but union negotiators still make common mistakes that hinder the development of agreements and compromises. These mistakes include those listed below.

Failing to plan

Plans need to be in place to properly reach an agreement. These plans should account for everything that might happen. While this might appear to be a daunting task, it is doable.

Many union negotiators forget about or ignore the following factors that need to be a part of planning:

Research

Research compares similar cases for contrast and comparison purposes. Smart union planners think about the following question regarding research:

> What were some similar union negotiations, what were the outcomes, and how do they relate to this negotiation?

Agenda

Agenda determines the basic strategy of the meeting. Smart union planners think about the following question regarding agenda:

> What issues are top priorities for each side, how much emphasis should be put on each of these, and when should they be discussed?

Goals

Goals are the desired objectives of each side. Smart union planners think about the following question regarding goals:

> What are the goals for each side, what are acceptable outcomes, and what are unacceptable outcomes?

Options

Options are solutions to a failed negotiation. Smart union planners think about the following question regarding alternatives:

> What direction will be taken if an agreement is not reached and how can good working relationships be maintained?

Failing to listen or observe

Please consider the following for these two mistakes:

Listening

As noted earlier, some union negotiators would rather hear themselves talk than listen to what the other side has to say. This can impact the outcome of negotiations...even to a point where an agreement cannot be reached. A lot more is learned by listening than talking, but some people fail to understand this fact.

Some union negotiators fail to pick up on non-verbal actions from the other side. Slouched body posture, crossed arms, smiles, raised eyebrows, and head shakes are all movements that can indicate people's thoughts. This information can then be used to find common ground and reach compromises.

Failing to keep an open mind

As noted earlier, union negotiators need open minds for finding alternative ways to reach an agreement. However, some people are unable to think "outside of the box," and this limits their options for problem-solving.

Open-minded thinking has been a critical aspect of research, innovation, and creativity for centuries. The same philosophy needs to be applied to negotiation...but this is something that many people fail to realize.

Failing to recognize one's behavior

Some union negotiators do not realize the impact of their behavior during negotiations. They need to understand that their actions are perceived by the other party in different ways...and negative perceptions can prevent an agreement from being reached.

Consider the following examples of behavior in negotiations:

- Loud people appear dominant. The other side views them as rude and aggressive.

- Quiet people appear aloof. The other side views them as having limited interest.
- Nervous people appear unprepared or inexperienced. The other side views them as having limited knowledge.
- People who do not make eye contact appear shady. The other side views them as untrustworthy.

In short, union negotiators who do not recognize the impact of their behavior are damaging to themselves and their members.

Failing to hold composure

One last mistake that is often not thought about involves the aftermath of negotiations. Some people celebrate the "victory" after the negotiation is over, and this response risks alienating the other side.

Gloating is unprofessional and it makes the other side seek revenge in future negotiations. In short, union negotiators need to think about the impact of their reactions to the final agreement.

The road to obtaining negotiation experience can be a difficult one to navigate, and union representatives need help along the way. The following three suggestions provide some help to make that road a little easier:

Listen and observe

This book discusses listening and observation as important aspects of negotiation on several occasions. However, there is no overkill here because this point cannot be overemphasized for union negotiators.

Let's repeat one more time:

- Stop talking
- Listen to what the other side is saying
- Observe the other side's non-verbal behavior

The above three bullets improve union negotiators' skills immediately. They should try them to see for themselves how well they work.

Adjust

Union negotiators need to adjust their communication styles to meet the needs of the other side. This improvement technique expands on listening and observing by going a step further and reacting. They should react to what the other side is saying by responding in the same tone of voice and using similar mannerisms. Mirroring their responses makes them feel more comfortable.

Additionally, emotions need to be kept in check at all times. Nothing hurts agreements more than uncontrolled emotional outbursts.

Think of the other party as a customer who is being sold something. They need to be comfortable with the people on the other side of the negotiating table. If they are not comfortable, they will not buy what is being sold....and there will be no agreement.

Plan and prepare

Planning and preparation are areas that all union negotiators can improve upon if they want to invest the time and effort. Think about the following:

- There is more negotiation research that can be conducted for comparison and contrast purposes.
- There are better negotiation agendas that can be formulated.
- There are more options available for negotiations that fail.

People who disagree with the above statements do so because they think they have done enough to plan and prepare. However, they might find out that this is simply not the case after they enter into an important negotiation...and then it is too late.

Negotiation is an important topic of discussion for any book on union activities because it determines the amount and type of compensation that members will receive for their work efforts. The next section discusses compensation for a better understanding of what it is, how it works, and what it entails.

Pay and compensation

Employee compensation comes in many different forms including pay, retirement plans, profit-sharing, stock ownership, and benefits. Union employees want job satisfaction, and money always seems to play a role in finding that satisfaction. In fact, money is typically one of the most important aspects of employment, and it is a major reason why workers remain at their current employer or leave for other positions.

This section examines various types of pay structures and benefits for union employees. Specifically, it looks at hourly pay, piece-rate pay, profit-sharing programs, employee stock ownership programs, and benefit packages. Each type of compensation is described, discussed in terms of pros and cons, and illustrated using a workplace example as shown below.

Hourly

Union employees who are compensated hourly receive an agreed-upon amount of money per hour of work. There is no guaranteed amount of money that these employees make in a year because the number of hours worked depends on organizational needs or customer demand. However, unions have changed the rules for many workplaces by guaranteeing minimum hours per week for hourly employees.

Typically increases in money per hour for hourly employees are based on time intervals or the ability to perform certain job functions. Again, unions have intervened and implemented rules that need to be followed in some workplaces. These rules guarantee employees wage increases after a certain amount of time with the organization. Rarely do hourly wages go down, but this can happen if concessions are implemented.

Organizational example

Katrina is a union production worker at a forklift assembly plant, and she earns 14 dollars per hour. When she works over 40 hours in a week, she receives 21 dollars per hour. In short, Katrina's compensation is a pre-determined wage for every hour she works assembling forklifts.

Below are some pros and cons of hourly pay:

Employee advantages

- Hourly employees get paid overtime (typically 1.5 times their normal hourly wage) when they work more than 40 hours a week…and sometimes when they work more than eight hours a day. In this respect, they get paid for every minute they are on the job.

- In general, hourly employees have designated pay increases. For example, management might give them a raise after 90 days to show that they are valued. Unions are often used to guarantee higher wages for these workers, and management has no choice other than to comply once changes in compensation have been negotiated.

- Hourly workers often have less stressful jobs than salaried workers. They have designated work that they must perform, but that work is done under controlled conditions with established productivity requirements.

Employee disadvantages

- Hourly employees are usually required to punch a time clock. Every minute that they work is tracked, and they do not get paid if they are not punched in.

- Hourly employees find it difficult to budget their expenses because they do not know how much money they will earn in a pay period. They have to wait to see how many hours they worked and be concerned about making less money during slow periods.

- Hourly employees lack power. They often rank low in the hierarchy, and they have limited say in the direction of the organization. This can cause job dissatisfaction and lower morale.

Piece-rate

This form of compensation pays employees a pre-determined amount of money for a specific amount of work. Union employees earn income based on their total output regardless of the amount of time they spend doing the job.

Organizational example

Gary works as a union assembler at a cell phone company. He does not receive an hourly wage or a salary for his efforts. Instead, his entire compensation is based on the number of cell phones he assembles regardless of the amount of time it takes him.

Below are some pros and cons of piece-rate pay:

Employee advantages

- Piece-rate provides a unique opportunity for earning income. Workers who produce quickly can earn more money than people who are paid hourly to do the same work.

- Employees take pride in their productivity because they are responsible from start to finish. They do not need others to help them do their jobs.

- Less supervision is needed because employees know exactly what they need to do to accomplish tasks. Workers make all job-related decisions, and they essentially manage themselves.

Employee disadvantages

- Employees who move too quickly can lose focus on quality and end up producing inferior products. They know that slowing down costs them money, so they are willing to sacrifice quality for quantity.

- Piece-rate pay discourages teamwork because employees prefer to work alone to earn money for themselves. This prevents people from collaborating on new ideas and concepts.

- Piece-rate pay does not help employees build skills outside of speed and productivity. They cannot solve unique problems because their focus is limited.

Profit-sharing

This type of compensation is provided in addition to wages earned for work performed. It is based on the profitability of the organization, and the union might or might not be involved in determining the amount of the contribution. The money is often paid out when employees leave the organization or retire.

Organizational example

Maryanne is a union nurse at a private health care clinic. She earns an hourly wage and has a benefit package that includes health, dental, and life insurance. Additional compensation for Maryanne includes a profit-sharing retirement plan that the clinic contributes to after profitable years.

Below are some pros and cons of profit-sharing programs:

Employee advantages

- Profit-sharing plans are essentially free compensation. Employees have a retirement plan in place without contributing any of their own money.

- Profit-sharing plans promote teamwork. Employees work together and focus on making the organization profitable because they share in the rewards.

- Profit-sharing plans help employees identify with the organization. Employees feel like they are an active part of the company because their contributions matter.

Employee disadvantages

- Employees have a retirement plan in place that does not consist of their own money, but they do not determine the amount and time of the contributions. There is also no guarantee that contributions will be made.

- Employees sometimes focus only on profitability… regardless of the consequences. Lower quality or less expensive products might be more profitable in the short term, but they can have long-term ramifications that negatively impact the organization.

- Profit-sharing plans can be demotivating when contributions are not made. People become dependent on these plans for their retirement, and they lose morale when the organization chooses not to contribute.

Employee stock ownership

This type of compensation is part of a benefit program where employees can purchase stock. The price of the stock is typically below the market value, and this makes it easier to purchase for workers.

Organizational example

Brenda is a union electrician at an automotive supplier. She is paid an hourly wage and has medical and dental benefits for her family. Felicia also has an opportunity to own part of the company. Every year, her employer offers her the option to buy company stock at 20 percent below the market value. The only stipulation is that this stock cannot be sold until she leaves the company or retires.

Below are some pros and cons of employee stock ownership programs:

Employee advantages

- Employees are interested in the success of the company because they are stock owners. In short, they have a financial interest and want to see it grow.

- Employees tend to become more motivated when they own stock. They want to get involved in ways that help the company grow and prosper because they identify with it through ownership.

- Stock value grows as the organization grows. Employees can accrue large amounts of money as the value of their investment increases. Best of all, they can do this without the stress or headaches of managing the company.

Employee disadvantages

- Stock ownership is not always enough for employees to stay motivated. They also need to be informed of the company's status and progress to feel involved, and sometimes management fails to address this concern.

- Stock ownership programs are often designated for retirement. If the company performs poorly and the value of the stock decreases, then employees who relied on it for their retirement can end up with little or nothing.

- Often the stock issued to employees is non-voting in status. This means employees own stock, but they have no voice in the direction of the company.

Benefits

Employee benefits are compensation in addition to an agreed-upon wage. They encompass a variety of different components and are based on many factors. However, the major benefits referred to in this section are health insurance, dental insurance, life insurance, vacation, paid days off, and retirement programs.

Organizational example

Quinton just accepted a union carpenter at a construction company that builds arenas and stadiums. He will receive an hourly wage and a benefit package as additional compensation. This package includes health insurance, dental insurance, life insurance, two weeks of paid vacation, three paid days off, and a 401K program with a 25 percent company match.

Below are some pros and cons of benefit packages:

Employee advantages

- Benefit packages often allow employees to make choices, and this is good because people have different needs. They can select the benefits that are most beneficial and pass on the ones that are not essential.

- Good benefit packages are an added incentive to remain with an organization. In fact, benefits are more important than wages for some employees.

- Benefit packages allow employees to monitor and maintain the health of themselves and their families. This is good for the employee and the employer.

- Benefit packages often allow employees to make choices based on their needs, but the wrong choice can create financial problems. Quite simply, it is hard for employees to know what benefits will be needed in the future.

- Good benefit packages can force employees to stay at jobs that they dislike. They might want to move on to something that pays a higher wage or is more interesting, but they cannot make a change because they need the benefits offered by their current employer.

- The costs of benefits are constantly rising for organizations, and they need to pass some of this on to the employees. This means employees are required to pay for their benefits, and some opt out if they cannot afford to do so. When this happens, the benefits offered by the organization are no longer beneficial to the employee.

Work-life balance

Union leaders try to make the lives of their members better and this involves more than pay and benefits. It also involves happiness at home and on the job, and that happiness begins with work-life balance. Quite simply, workers who find this balance are happier in their personal and professional lives.

Work-life balance involves accomplishing work-related goals while enjoying life outside of work. As people's lives become busier and more hectic, they begin to realize the importance of work-life balance. Time is limited, and different things need to take priority at different times in life. People need to work to sustain a certain lifestyle, but they also need the time to enjoy that lifestyle.

Organizational example

Jacquelyn works as a union orderly at a hospital. The hospital has a work-life balance program in place where trained counselors are available to listen to the problems the hospital employees are experiencing at home or work. This program provides employees with someone who acts as a sounding board and offers advice when needed...and it helps Jacquelyn cope with the stress of her job.

Below are some pros and cons of work-life balance programs:

Employee advantages

- Stress is reduced. Work-life balance programs such as counseling and therapy help relieve stress and prevent the consequences that result from it.

- Physical health is improved. Gym memberships and exercise areas help employees maintain physical health at work and home.

- Telecommuting is a huge benefit for many employees. They can perform their job from home and not have to worry about traffic or restrictive work schedules.

Employee disadvantages

- Career progression is hampered. Telecommuters who are not involved in the day-to-day activities of the organization can be passed up by others simply because they are not physically noticed. This is a major concern for employees whose jobs are completely remote.

- Telecommuting can cause communication issues. Typically the major form of communication for employees working remotely is the written word (email, text, and letter)...and written words can easily be misinterpreted.

- Cost is a concern. Expenses can force organizations to eliminate work-life balance programs, and the loss of these programs can be demotivating to the employees who found them useful.

Now you have an understanding of the basic types of pay and compensation available for union employees. Union leaders need to figure out which types work best for their members to keep them content and productive. Ultimately, this requires finding and maintaining a balance between satisfied workers and a financially stable organization.

Summary

Labor unions have been a hot topic of discussion in the United States for many years because once voted in, they have sole authority to negotiate all conditions of employment for their members. They represent members in matters involving wages, benefits, working conditions, and disagreements with management over contract stipulations. Although unions have lost some power in recent years, they are still fairly common in organizations across the United States.

Below are some of the advantages and disadvantages of unionized workplaces from an employee perspective.

Advantages

Better wages and benefits

Unions fight for improved wages and benefits for their members. This often results in better compensation packages than workers who perform similar jobs in non-union plants.

Right to grievances

Union employees have the right to argue their position if they feel they have been wronged by the company. They simply file a grievance with the union steward, and the union fights on their behalf. Employees in non-union companies do not always have the option to argue their position because management's decision is final.

Strength in numbers

Unions have an advantage based on the number of members they have fighting for a common cause. In short, it's easier for a group of people to get a company to change than it is for any single person.

Secured jobs

Management in union companies cannot fire workers for any reason. A strict protocol must be followed to terminate an employee, and this provides job security for union members.

Disadvantages

Devaluation of high performers

Many people believe that higher-performing employees deserve higher pay. This is not possible in a union environment because workers at the same level are compensated equally.

Abuse

Unions were necessary when workers started to organize many years ago. Workplace conditions were often terrible, and management had no restrictions on how employees were treated. However, those types of workplace conditions are few and far between in the modern world because laws are in place to prevent them from existing. Today's unions often end up fighting for those members who abuse their protection. Some union employees are aware that companies have great difficulty firing them, and because of this, they abuse the system so it works to their advantage.

Problems with seniority

Unions reward employees based on seniority. Skills and qualifications are not taken into account when positions become available, and this means the best people are not always chosen for the job.

Loss of jobs

Unions do a good job of increasing wages and benefits for their members. However, these increases can put financial burdens on companies that cannot be overcome. When companies shut down because they are no longer profitable, everyone loses...including union members.

The above advantage and disadvantages could be argued and debated, but they do harness some people's thoughts about unionized workforces.

In a nutshell, this book helps readers gain an understanding of unions. It discusses union types, structures, activities, and functions while analyzing the role that they play for their members. It does not support or oppose unions in workplaces, nor does it argue the topic from any perspective. The goal is simply to educate readers about unions so they can formulate their own opinions.

Congratulations! You now understand more about labor unions...an important and influential aspect of workplaces all over the United States of America.